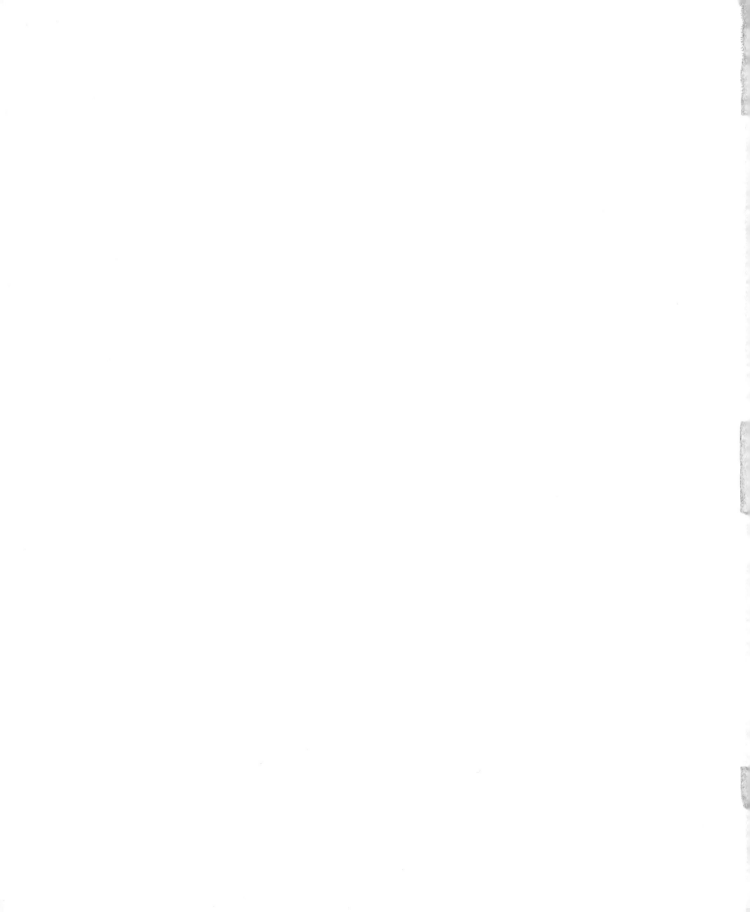

Chemical World

SCIENCE IN OUR DAILY LIVES

ROWENA RAE

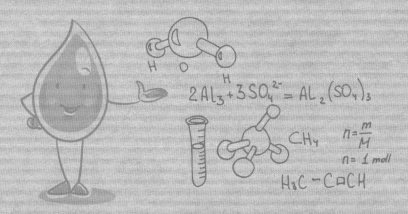

ORCA BOOK PUBLISHERS

Library and Archives Canada Cataloguing in Publication
Title: Chemical world : science in our daily lives / Rowena Rae.
Names: Rae, Rowena, author.
Series: Orca footprints.
Description: Series statement: Orca footprints | Includes bibliographical references and index.
Identifiers: Canadiana (print) 20190177632 | Canadiana (ebook) 20190177640 | ISBN 9781459821576 (hardcover) | ISBN 9781459821583 (PDF) | ISBN 9781459821590 (EPUB)
Subjects: LCSH: Chemistry—Juvenile literature. | LCSH: Chemicals—Juvenile literature.
Classification: LCC QD35 .R34 2020 | DDC j540—DC23
Issued in print and electronic formats.
ISBN 9781459821576 (hardcover) | ISBN 9781459821590 (PDF) | ISBN 9781459821583 (EPUB)

Library of Congress Control Number: 2019947376
Simultaneously published in Canada and the United States in 2020

Summary: Part of the nonfiction Footprints series for middle readers, this book examines the good and the bad of the chemicals we come into contact with in our daily lives.

Orca Book Publishers is committed to reducing the consumption of nonrenewable resources in the production of our books. We make every effort to use materials that support a sustainable future.

Orca Book Publishers gratefully acknowledges the support for its publishing programs provided by the following agencies: the Government of Canada, the Canada Council for the Arts and the Province of British Columbia through the BC Arts Council and the Book Publishing Tax Credit.

The author and publisher have made every effort to ensure that the information in this book was correct at the time of publication. The author and publisher do not assume any liability for any loss, damage or disruption caused by errors or omissions. Every effort has been made to trace copyright holders and to obtain their permission for the use of copyrighted material. The publisher apologizes for any errors or omissions and would be grateful if notified of any corrections that should be incorporated in future reprints or editions of this book.

Front cover photos: (top) Steve Debenport/Getty Images (bottom) Hero Images/Getty Images
Back cover photos: cglade/istock.com, Seneesriyota/dreamstime.com, Monkey Business Images/shutterstock.com

Edited by Sarah N. Harvey
Design and production by Teresa Bubela and Jenn Playford

ORCA BOOK PUBLISHERS
orcabook.com

Printed and bound in South Korea.

23 22 21 20 • 4 3 2 1

Water is made up of two chemical elements: hydrogen and oxygen. Without these elements and many others, life as we know it wouldn't exist on Earth. CASEZY IDEA/SHUTTERSTOCK.COM

For the children in my world:
Madeleine, Tristan, Genevieve, Luke and Melissa

Contents

CHAPTER THREE:
BLACK CLOUDS GATHERING

CHAPTER FOUR:
A SILVER LINING

Introduction

How does your morning routine go? Mine goes like this: Drink a cup of tea, shampoo and condition my hair, apply lotion and makeup, get dressed, eat cereal with milk and apple slices, brush teeth. Ready for the day ahead!

I never used to think about the products I lather on my hair and rub into my skin every morning, but recently I squinted at the shampoo bottle. It had an awfully long list of ingredients. What are all those impossible-to-pronounce words?

Of course I know they're **chemicals**. After all, everything on our planet is made of chemicals. Chemicals are simply groups of basic **elements** like carbon, oxygen, nitrogen and 115 others. I'm made of chemicals, and so are you and anything you can touch, taste, hear, see or smell—and even some things our senses can't detect.

But what are all those chemicals doing in my shampoo? Do any of them harm me while they're cleaning my hair? Do any of them harm the environment after they wash down the drain? Same for the lotion, the makeup, the toothpaste.

Me with my breakfast. GENEVIEVE WILSON

We all need food to live, grow and learn. What goes into our bodies each time we eat? MARTINEDOUCET/ISTOCK.COM

And then there's my breakfast. What am I putting inside my body each time I eat or drink? Was the environment harmed while the ingredients were being grown or processed? What about the things I toss out—the tea bag, the apple core, the empty plastic milk jug? Does my household waste cause problems for the environment?

I decided to learn more about environmental chemistry and all the chemicals I interact with every day. I found out some fascinating things, some sad things and some alarming things too. The good, the bad and the unknown.

Grab a drink—maybe a nice glass of hydrogen and oxygen in the form of water—and I'll tell you more.

CHAPTER ONE

A Chemical History Tour

Fire is a chemical reaction known as combustion.
EVDOHA_SPB/SHUTTERSTOCK.COM

WAIT! WHAT'S A CHEMICAL AGAIN?

If you're not sure, you're not alone. Many of us are a bit fuzzy when it comes to understanding chemicals. As I said before, a chemical is a bunch of basic elements joined together. Look at the periodic table of elements. Different combinations of these basic elements make up everything on Earth.

Every living thing has four main elements—carbon, hydrogen, oxygen and nitrogen. On the periodic table find the letter for each one. Put the letters together, and it's easy to remember that every living thing—from red-tide algae to an elephant—is made of the four elements that spell CHON. Living things contain small amounts of other elements too.

Nonliving things—like water, air and rocks—are also made of basic elements. Water has hydrogen and oxygen. Air (at least, the air we breathe on Earth) has nitrogen, oxygen, argon and tiny amounts of several other elements. And rocks—well, rocks come in lots of chemical combinations. For example, limestone

8

Periodic Table of the Elements

1	2	3	4	5	6	7	8	9	10	11	12	13	14	15	16	17	18
H Hydrogen																	He
Li	Be											B	C Carbon	N Nitrogen	O Oxygen	F Fluorine	Ne
Na Sodium	Mg											Al Aluminum	Si Silicon	P Phosphorus	S Sulfur	Cl Chlorine	Ar Argon
K	Ca Calcium	Sc	Ti Titanium	V	Cr	Mn	Fe Iron	Co Cobalt	Ni	Cu Copper	Zn Zinc	Ga	Ge	As Arsenic	Se	Br	Kr
Rb	Sr	Y	Zr	Nb	Mo	Tc	Ru	Rh	Pd	Ag Silver	Cd Cadmium	In	Sn Tin	Sb	Te	I	Xe
Cs	Ba	La	Hf	Ta	W	Re	Os	Ir	Pt	Au Gold	Hg Mercury	Tl	Pb Lead	Bi	Po	At	Rn
Fr	Ra	Ac	Rf	Db	Sg	Bh	Hs	Mt	Ds	Rg	Cn	Nh	Fl	Mc	Lv	Ts	Og

Ce	Pr	Nd	Pm	Sm	Eu	Gd	Tb	Dy	Ho	Er	Tm	Yb	Lu
Th	Pa	U	Np	Pu	Am	Cm	Bk	Cf	Es	Fm	Md	No	Lr

The periodic table of elements. The elements were first placed in this arrangement in the 1870s by Russian chemist Dmitri Mendeleev. ROWENA RAE

has calcium, carbon and oxygen. Granite rocks are silicon, oxygen and other elements.

But this isn't a book about rocks, so let's move on to a burning question.

TAMING FIRE

Imagine a family of cave dwellers huddled in their cave, eating raw meat. They are made of chemicals and so is everything around them—the cave walls, the meat, the bed of dried grass. Suddenly a spark blows into the cave from a nearby wildfire and *whoosh!* The grass catches on fire.

Why are we talking about fire? Fire is an example of a **chemical reaction**. In a chemical reaction, one or more chemicals transform, or change, into one or more different chemicals. In fire's case, a fuel (such as grass) plus oxygen in the air get kick-started by a spark and transform into carbon dioxide plus water. As this transformation happens, heat and particles (smoke and soot, for example) are released.

IT'S ELEMENTAL: Of the 118 elements on the periodic table, 92 are found in nature. The rest are made by humans.

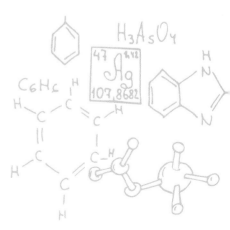

Early humans would have known about fire from wild-fires and volcanoes before they knew how to make or control fire themselves. Archaeologists—scientists who study human history—have found old fire pits, ashes and other evidence showing that people started making fires deliberately at least 700,000 years ago. As well as warmth and cooked food, fire gave people a place to gather and socialize. Knowing how to light a fire was an important step in human evolution. Fires were also one of the earliest types of pollution.

MIXED METALS

Early humans used stones and bones as tools. Then they started working metals like copper and tin—also basic elements—into spear tips, knives and bowls. Later humans found a way to mix copper and tin to make a new, strong metal called bronze. Bronze is an **alloy**, meaning that basic elements have been melted together in a **physical reaction**, not a chemical one. The basic elements are still there but in a new arrangement.

Here's a way to remember the difference. In a physical reaction, you can get the original ingredients back as individual things. For example, when you spread jam on bread, the jam is still jam and the bread is still bread. In a chemical reaction, the original ingredients change into something new and you *cannot* get them back. For example, when you cook an egg, the gloppy white and runny yolk become firm. You can't get the original white and yolk back. Seems like magic, but it's chemistry.

THE ALCHEMIST'S MYSTICAL LAIR

Have you read the first Harry Potter book? If so, you'll remember the philosopher's stone (or sorcerer's stone, depending on where you live). This stone turned metal into gold and produced a liquid giving immortality (eternal life) to the person who drank it. Author J.K. Rowling created a fantasy world, but did

These ax heads found in present-day Hungary date to the years 2000–600 BCE, which are within the time frame of the Bronze Age.
BRIDGEMANIMAGES.COM

An Iranian painting of alchemists from 1893.
BRIDGEMANIMAGES.COM

you know that the idea of the philosopher's stone is true? In Rowling's novel, an alchemist named Nicolas Flamel created the stone. In real life, alchemy was an early form of chemistry. There was a real Nicolas Flamel too. He lived in France in the 1300s and 1400s. Centuries after his death he became known as an alchemist, but there is no evidence that he really was one.

Real-life alchemists tried to transform metals into gold, discover a medicine to heal all ills and create an "elixir of life" to give humans immortality. Alchemists didn't achieve any of these goals, but they still made discoveries. They found elements like phosphorus and zinc, and they created mixtures like gunpowder (the first explosive).

Over time, people's thinking began to shift away from alchemy, and by the late 1700s, modern chemistry had largely taken its place.

IT'S ELEMENTAL: Clay is a soft material made up of the basic elements silicon, aluminum, oxygen, hydrogen and others. When clay is heated to very high temperatures, it goes through a series of chemical reactions that burn off some elements and rearrange the connections among other elements, eventually turning the soft clay into a hard ceramic. Shards of ancient pottery have been found in China and date to about 20,000 years ago.

CHEMICAL CONCOCTIONS

Throughout the 1800s, chemists discovered many new materials and mixtures, which gave society many exciting items. Here are a few examples:
- Iron or steel containers lined with tin became the first tin cans, capable of preserving food.
- Vulcanized or cured rubber—created by heating the thick sap of rubber trees together with sulfur—made flexible items like hoses, shoe soles, waterproof clothing and, later, car tires.
- Kerosene, an oil refined from coal and shale, replaced smelly whale oil in lamps.

THE AGE OF PLASTICS

Do you know what else was first made in the mid-1800s? I bet you're using or wearing something made of it right now. Plastic!

Can you imagine a world without plastic? After all, it's everywhere—in furniture, clothing, drinking bottles...

A boy holds up a kerosene lamp.
VALERIY MINYAEV/DREAMSTIME.COM

Mauveine was the first synthetic dye. It was discovered accidentally by a British chemistry student, William Henry Perkin, and allowed ordinary people (not just royalty) to afford purple clothing.

COURTESY OF THE SCIENCE HISTORY INSTITUTE

What fun to work with these

NEW MOTHER'S HELPERS

LIGHT, SO SMOOTH, SO PLIABLE . . .

BAKELITE
BRAND
Polyethylene Plastic

A 1950s magazine advertisement for Bakelite. BRIDGEMANIMAGES.COM

How did people ever live without it? Well, only 150 years ago they did. Furniture was made of wood, clothing of natural fibers like cotton and wool, and bottles of glass.

In the 1850s a British chemist made the first plastic—a material with the characteristic of plasticity, meaning it could be molded into a particular shape. Called Parkesine, it wasn't very useful. Soon afterward a better plastic was made as a substitute for elephant ivory in billiard balls. Billiards, which is a game similar to pool, had become popular and manufacturers wanted a cheaper material for making the balls. American chemist John Wesley Hyatt experimented with cellulose, the natural material that gives trees structure. The result was called celluloid, and it made a suitable substitute for ivory in billiard balls. Well, suitable most of the time. Celluloid billiard balls had a habit of exploding when they smacked together (which happens in billiards). Celluloid was flammable, meaning it could easily catch on fire. Nevertheless, celluloid plastic found its way into everyday items, such as combs, toothbrush handles, toys and detachable shirt collars (yes, those were everyday items in the late 1800s).

The next advance in plastics came in 1907, when Leo Baekeland, a Belgian American chemist, mixed phenol (from coal tar) with formaldehyde (a wood alcohol). He invented a **synthetic** (or human-made) plastic that could be molded into a shape and then set with heat. Called Bakelite, this plastic could be used to make everything from bracelets to telephones.

Bakelite has since been replaced by many other types of synthetic plastic. They can be transparent like plastic wrap, soft like squeaky toys, threads like nylon stockings, hard but breakable like a lunch box or hard and strong like underground pipes.

Most plastics have one thing in common—they're made from **petroleum**. Sometimes called "rock oil" or "crude oil," this natural substance is also the starting point for making gasoline, kerosene and other fuels.

Large-scale plastic production took off after World War II, which ended in 1945. Since then humans have produced more than eight billion tons of plastic! Plastic pollution has become an immense problem on land and in the oceans. But that's the subject of a whole other book.

PESTS, BE GONE!

Other inventions from the chemist's lab became part of everyday life after World War II too. Have you ever heard of DDT? It's a synthetic chemical with a crazy-long name (dichlorodiphenyl-trichloroethane—try saying that ten times fast!). A chemist first made DDT in 1874 but couldn't find a use for it. Then in 1939 Paul Müller, a Swiss chemist, discovered that DDT killed house flies. He realized the chemical was a strong **pesticide** (-*cide* is Latin for "cut" or "kill") and could control pests, such as lice and mosquitoes.

During World War II, people in Naples, Italy, lined up to have DDT powder sprinkled in their hair, up their shirts and down their pants. The aim was to stop an outbreak of typhus. Bacteria cause this disease, and lice carry the bacteria. The people-powdering worked! DDT killed the lice, and typhus didn't spread. But it wasn't yet known that DDT has other less-positive effects.

After the war DDT went into all sorts of products so people could kill bugs easily at home. Sprays to blast into closets, powders to sprinkle on pets, even wallpaper to decorate children's bedrooms. DDT was also used to kill mosquitoes carrying malaria, a terrible disease. Trucks sprayed DDT along residential streets, at public beaches and in parks, even while people played and ate picnics.

Airplanes sprayed DDT over agricultural crops too. It and other pesticides seemed like wonder products to farmers battling weevils, moths and other crop-destroying pests. DDT had the advantage of staying in the environment for a long time. One spraying could last in the environment for six months. This, it later turned out, is one of the problems with DDT.

IT'S ELEMENTAL: The human body has about 60 basic elements in it. At least half of these are necessary to keep our bodies in good working order.

A man is dusted with DDT powder to stop the spread of disease-carrying insects.
BRIDGEMANIMAGES.COM

IT'S ELEMENTAL: Some mosquito species have become resistant to pesticides. They have developed ways to be unaffected by DDT and other pesticides.

WHAT'S THIS ONE FOR?

Chemicals, both natural and synthetic, are in the things we use every day. But why is a particular chemical in a particular product? They aren't there just because chemists had fun finding or synthesizing (making) them. They have a purpose. Here are a few examples:

- Flame retardants prevent fire from starting or slow the spread of flames. They're in electronics, furniture (such as couches and mattresses) and building materials (such as electrical wires and insulation).
- Metals added to paints and plastics give color: yellow, orange and red from cadmium, green from copper and arsenic, blue from cobalt and white from titanium.
- Parabens in cosmetics (makeup) and medicines act as preservatives.
- Phthalates (THAL-ates) make plastics softer and flexible. They're also added to shampoo, lotion and soap as fragrances.

Many vibrant paint colors come from metals. CHAMILLE WHITE/SHUTTERSTOCK.COM

My Chemical World

As a university student I was invited to spend a month in Antarctica to do biology research. I leaped at the chance. While there I visited some historic sites, including the Cape Royds hut, built by Ernest Shackleton and his British Antarctic Expedition in 1908. When these explorers sailed home a year later, they left some things behind. Eighty-eight years later, as I stood in the dim interior, it struck me how not a single thing was made of plastic. I saw wooden crates, metal food boxes, glass bottles and paper wrappers, but no plastic.

The explorers left a lot behind in their hut, but not a single thing was plastic.
ROWENA RAE

- Stabilizers keep plastics from getting damaged by heat or light. Other stabilizers keep foods the right consistency and color.
- Surfactants (surface active agents) in cookware, food packaging and fabrics resist grease and water. Other surfactants in detergents and shampoos help "lift" grease.
- Antibacterials in toothpaste and soap kill bacteria.

WONDERFUL OR WORRISOME?

Many exciting chemical discoveries have given us a mind-boggling array of options each time we go to buy toothpaste, a water bottle, an apple or any of thousands of other items.

But are all these products truly wonderful? Do any of the chemicals in them (or on them) harm people or the environment, even if harm wasn't the intention?

Before looking more closely at these questions, let's talk a little more about where chemicals come from, how chemists refer to them and what happens to them in the environment. Join me for some chemical alphabet soup.

A man sells plastic of every shape and color at an outdoor market.
SAURAV PURKAYASTHA/DREAMSTIME.COM

My Chemical World

I love making pottery. At one studio we had big pails of color glazes to dip our pots into. The glazes were mixtures of all sorts of pigments and other chemicals, which would separate—heavier particles sank when the glazes sat unused for a while. We'd roll up our sleeves and plunge our bare arms into the pails to stir the glazes. I remember scraping my fingernails along the bottom of the pails to get the sediments mixed back in. I now know that those sediments included metals like cadmium and cobalt. What I'll never know is how much of these and other chemicals I absorbed through my skin while I stirred the glazes, and whether they'll cause me any harm. But I wonder.

It's safer to glaze pots by holding them with tongs.
DRAGONIMAGES/ISTOCK.COM

CHAPTER TWO

Alphabet Soup

THE WORLD'S BEST CHEMIST

Nature is the first and ultimate chemist. As you read in chapter 1, *everything* consists of basic elements joined in different ways.

Living things—those with CHON—are called **organic**. This includes dead things that once were living, like fossilized plants and animals. Therefore, in chemistry, *organic* includes petroleum—the remains of millennia-old algae, plants and other organisms. Petroleum is the starting point for making gasoline, natural gas and plastic. These are all petroleum products.

Just to be confusing, the term *organic* is also used for food grown without certain fertilizers, pesticides and hormones. The thing is, even non-organic (conventionally farmed) food is made of organic chemicals.

Nonliving things like water, air and rocks are not organic— termed **inorganic**. They are also made of basic elements.

Petroleum, or crude oil, is often deep brown or black. PIX ONE/SHUTTERSTOCK.COM

A view of organisms (which are organic, in the chemical sense) in a tide pool created by rocks (inorganic) and filled with water (also inorganic).
ROWENA RAE

SYNTHETICS GALORE

When humans make chemicals using different methods than nature's, the result is called a synthetic chemical. Vitamin C in an orange is nature's chemical, and vitamin C made by chemists as a food additive is synthetic.

Fibers for clothing can be natural or synthetic too. Nature's fibers include cotton (from cotton plants), silk (from silkworms) and wool (from sheep). Chemists make fibers like nylon and polyester, both from—yup—petroleum, *again*.

Estimates vary for how many different synthetic chemicals have been created. The Environmental Protection Agency (EPA) records all the chemicals made in or imported into the United States. It lists about 85,000 chemicals.

TONGUE-TWISTER NAMES

Are you having trouble pronouncing some of the chemical names in this book? I certainly have! Many names are long and complex, because they identify the elements in a chemical and their relationship to each other. Remember the pesticide introduced in chapter 1, dichlorodiphenyltrichloroethane or DDT, which was sprayed to kill insects? It has 14 carbon, 9 hydrogen and 5 chlorine atoms (the smallest parts of a chemical element) joined in a specific structure.

Other chemicals are named for their shape. *Basketane* looks like a basket and *penguinone* like a penguin. Still others are named after characters, such as *pikachurin* for the Pokémon Pikachu.

Groups of related chemicals also get complicated names, like polychlorinated biphenyls (PCBs) and chlorofluorocarbons (CFCs). You don't need to remember the long names, but look for some of the abbreviations later in this book.

Tricky names aside, a myth we need to bury right away is that *natural* chemicals are good and *synthetic* ones are bad.

Chemists have created thousands of different synthetic chemicals using equipment like these students have in their chemistry lab.

MONKEY BUSINESS IMAGES/SHUTTERSTOCK.COM

IT'S ELEMENTAL: Chemical engineer Robert Gore invented Gore-Tex by accident. He was in his lab, working on an experiment. Frustrated by how it was going, he yanked on a rod of heated polytetrafluoroethylene (PTFE, also known as Teflon). The rod stretched by 800 percent into a strong, lightweight, waterproof material. Gore-Tex has many uses, including clothing, medical devices and even textiles for space exploration.

ARE ALL NATURAL CHEMICALS GOOD?

No way. Not by a long shot!

Many people see the word *natural* on a product and assume it must be safe and healthy. But that's a dangerous assumption, because all sorts of living and nonliving things found in nature—making them "natural"—are in fact poisonous.

TOXIC TENDENCIES

A plant called curare, native to South America, contains **toxic chemicals** (or **toxicants**). Indigenous Peoples in the Amazon region make a paste from the plant's bark and smear it on arrows. Animals shot with a ***poison*** arrow quickly become paralyzed and die. In the 1940s doctors started using small amounts of curare to relax patients' muscles, especially during surgery. Synthetic versions of curare are also in some modern drugs.

Why would a plant contain a deadly poison? Many plants and animals use toxic chemicals as a defense against being eaten. Other living things with chemical defenses include poison ivy (the name gives it away!), foxgloves, box jellyfish, monarch butterflies, black widow spiders—the list could fill pages.

It's pretty scary to think about all these toxic plants and animals. But stay calm! The chances of being poisoned in nature are low, because we learn not to touch poisonous things and especially never to eat something unless we know for sure it's safe.

MAD AS A HATTER

Among poisonous nonliving things are the elements arsenic, lead and mercury. Mercury is an interesting one. It's the only metal that stays liquid at room temperature. Mercury rolling on a surface looks like silvery water droplets beading on a dewy leaf. Mercury is beautiful but also highly poisonous.

This mushroom's name—death cap—gives away the fact that it contains a deadly toxin. Its scientific name is Amanita phalloides.
VOLODYMYR NIKITENKO/SHUTTERSTOCK.COM

IT'S ELEMENTAL: Planet Earth can never be completely free of pollution, since even natural forces like wildfires, volcanic eruptions and lightning strikes cause pollution.

The bright colors of a poison dart frog warn predators to stay away or risk being poisoned. PUG1979/DREAMSTIME.COM

Teatime for Alice, the White Rabbit, the Dormouse and the Hatter—a character who may have been inspired by hat makers who suffered from mercury poisoning.
MORPHART CREATION/SHUTTERSTOCK.COM

In the 1800s and into the 1900s, hat makers used a mercury solution in their work, and many developed what became known as Mad Hatter disease—strange behaviors, slurred speech and tremors (called "hatter's shakes"). This disease and its name may have been Lewis Carroll's inspiration for the character of the Hatter, described by the Cheshire Cat as "mad" in the book *Alice's Adventures in Wonderland*.

CLIMBING THE FOOD CHAIN

You've probably heard about **food chains**. At the base of all food chains are plants or algae. They get eaten by **herbivores**, the plant eaters, who get eaten by **carnivores**, the meat eaters. All carnivores are **predators**, and the animals at the top of a food chain are the **apex predators**.

This is a simple food chain: clover (plant), eaten by rabbit (herbivore), eaten by fox (carnivore and predator), eaten by hawk (carnivore and apex predator).

Being at the top of your food chain has pros and cons. The pro is not having other animals constantly trying to eat you. The con is being on the losing end of **biomagnification**.

This osprey—an apex predator—has lunch in its talons. VLADIMIR KOGAN MICHAEL/SHUTTERSTOCK.COM

Toxic Terms

These words are similar but not quite the same:

Poison: Any natural or synthetic substance that causes illness or death

Toxin: A natural poison that comes from a plant or animal

Toxic chemical (or toxicant): Any poisonous substance, whether natural or synthetic

Pollutant: A natural or synthetic substance that makes the environment (air, water or soil) dirty or impure

Contaminant: A natural or synthetic substance that makes either the environment or a living organism dirty or impure

An image of a skull and crossbones has been used since the 1800s to identify poisonous substances.
GWENGOAT/ISTOCK.COM

To picture how biomagnification happens, let's go up that food chain again, this time in a meadow with chemical **contaminants** in the soil. The clover's roots absorb some soil contaminants, which accumulate (build up) in the clover leaves. Each next level accumulates more than the previous level had. The rabbits accumulate more chemical contaminants per individual than each clover plant had. The foxes accumulate more per individual than each rabbit had. The hawks end up with the most chemical contaminants in their bodies.

Hold this picture of biomagnification at work while you read about a tragic episode in environmental history.

MYSTERIOUS ILLNESS

In 1956 a baby girl was born in a Japanese fishing village on Minamata Bay. Shinobu Sakamoto grew slowly. At three months old she couldn't hold up her head. At three years old she couldn't walk. Doctors diagnosed cerebral palsy, where the body's muscles are uncoordinated. But other local children also had health problems and so did animals. Fish swam oddly, seabirds couldn't fly and cats convulsed with "dancing disease."

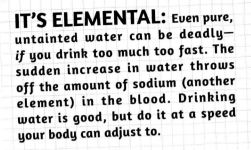

IT'S ELEMENTAL: Even pure, untainted water can be deadly—if you drink too much too fast. The sudden increase in water throws off the amount of sodium (another element) in the blood. Drinking water is good, but do it at a speed your body can adjust to.

My Chemical World

When I was in the eighth or ninth grade, my chemistry teacher passed around a sample of mercury. Everyone in the class got to look at the mercury up close—and hold it too. I remember cupping the glob of silver-colored liquid in my hand and watching it roll around as I moved my wrist. Mesmerizing. Little did I know—and my teacher must not have known either—how poisonous mercury is.

Mercury's symbol is Hg, from the Latin hydrargyrus. It's also called quicksilver.
WIEN-TIROL/SHUTTERSTOCK.COM

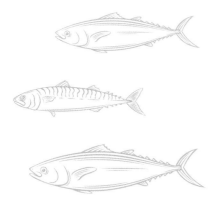

Shinobu didn't have cerebral palsy. She had mercury poisoning, passed to her unknowingly by her pregnant mother. More than 2,000 people in Minamata got mercury poisoning and became ill with such symptoms as numb hands and feet, weak muscles and damaged vision, hearing and speech.

How did the people get poisoned? From eating mercury-contaminated seafood. How did the seafood get contaminated? From mercury-filled waste dumped by a factory into Minamata Bay. The dumping had been going on since the 1930s, and over time mercury had entered the food chain and biomagnified from algae to shellfish to finfish to people.

Mercury contamination is a worldwide problem. Many marine fish, especially top predators like mackerel and tuna, have high amounts of mercury in their tissues. Mercury used to be widely used in thermometers, and it's still used in batteries, fluorescent light bulbs, some medical devices and other products. When these things break or are thrown away, the mercury evaporates and leaks out into the environment. A global treaty to phase out the use of mercury in most products came into effect in 2017, when Shinobu Sakamoto was 61. She traveled to Geneva, Switzerland, to attend a meeting of nations that had signed the treaty. Shinobu couldn't walk on her own and had difficulty speaking, but she urged the world to end mercury poisoning.

Being a top predator in the food chain, tuna often accumulate high levels of mercury. ZAFERKIZILKAY/SHUTTERSTOCK.COM

A LITTLE OR A LOT?

The expression "The dose makes the poison" means that sometimes (not always!) a small amount of a substance is harmless, but a larger amount is poisonous. For example, many fruit trees, including apple, cherry and peach, have a chemical called cyanide in their leaves and in the seeds or pits of their fruit. The fleshy part of the fruit can have trace (very small) amounts of cyanide, but they're so small that animals (including humans) aren't at risk of harm when they eat these fruits. At high doses, though, cyanide can affect breathing and heart function.

But it's important to realize that sometimes the dose *sounds* really small, but even that low dose is enough to do harm. You also have to think about *when* someone or something gets exposed to a chemical. For example, babies and young children are particularly vulnerable to low doses of chemicals because their bodies—especially their brains—are growing so rapidly.

I've mentioned a few examples of harm from natural chemicals. What about synthetic chemicals? For some people, the very word *synthetic* equates to "bad for us." But is that true? Read on.

ARE ALL SYNTHETIC CHEMICALS BAD?

No. Just because a chemical is made in a human lab instead of nature's lab doesn't mean it's harmful. Whether a chemical is poisonous for people or the environment comes down to two things: what it's made of (the elements it contains and how they're joined) and how it's used.

There are thousands of synthetic chemicals. The concerning part is that only a few hundred have been tested well enough to know whether they're safe for the environment and people.

As early as the 1940s and 1950s, people began asking questions. Was the rapid pace of making and using pesticides and other synthetic chemicals careless? Were some of them harmful, even if harm wasn't intended? Were we—and are we still—too accepting of new products without first considering their effects, both good and bad?

The next chapter offers answers to these questions. Some of the stories I write about are sad and upsetting, but I want to give you information that will help you understand the risks associated with some chemicals. I hope knowing more about chemical contaminants will lead you to look for solutions to the problems and play a part in protecting the environment and your own health.

IT'S ELEMENTAL: All rainwater is slightly acidic as a result of the carbonic acid in it (the product of a chemical reaction between carbon dioxide and water). When air pollutants emitted by factories and cars react with water, oxygen and other chemicals, they form sulfuric acid and nitric acid. These acids can then mix with water in the atmosphere to become "acid rain." When acid rain falls, it changes water and soil chemistry, which stresses and sometimes kills fish, trees and other organisms.

Factory emissions make rainwater more acidic. When it falls, acid rain harms the environment.
PAUL PRESCOTT/SHUTTERSTOCK.COM

CHAPTER THREE

Black Clouds Gathering

This bald eagle keeps a watchful eye on its eaglet. BEVERLY/SHUTTERSTOCK.COM

WHERE DID ALL THE EAGLES GO?

What did the bald eagle say to its friend before they went hunting for food?

"Let us **prey**."

About 50 years ago, some people began to pray (not prey!) for bald eagles. No joke. Eagles were in trouble—and so were other large birds, such as ospreys, hawks and pelicans.

In the 1700s as many as 200,000 bald eagles soared through the skies of North America. Yet in the early 1900s their numbers nose-dived. What was happening? At first human hunting and egg gathering were to blame.

Then another threat appeared—DDT. Remember how effective DDT was in halting the spread of disease-carrying lice? Well, it has a dark side. Once it gets into the environment, DDT accumulates and biomagnifies through food chains. As apex predators, bald eagles accumulated a heavy load of the chemical.

The DDT didn't appear to affect the adult birds though. Instead, it made their eggshells thinner. Picture eggs with thin, weak shells being sat on by heavy parent eagles. Result: *crack, splat.*

SILENT SPRING

Even before DDT came into common use after World War II, a few scientists and others questioned its safety. But it wasn't until a book about agricultural pesticides became a bestseller (yes, it really did!) that government officials and the public paid attention. The author was Rachel Carson, and her book was *Silent Spring.*

Published in 1962, this book warned about overuse and misuse of DDT and other pesticides. Carson described cases of severe illness and even death after people were exposed to certain agricultural and garden-care chemicals. She also wrote about animals keeling over dead, food chains being disrupted and ecosystems unraveling after being sprayed with pesticides. The book sparked controversy and received a lot of attention.

Within less than a decade many pesticides, DDT included, had been banned from use in the United States and Canada. In 2001 DDT was banned from agricultural use worldwide.

And the eagles? Since the DDT ban, the population has been on the upswing. Today tens of thousands of bald eagles again soar through the skies.

TRICKSTER CHEMICALS

Did you know there's an actual job that involves catching crocodiles and examining them to find out if they're male or female? Sounds a bit dangerous! But some biologists do just that. With their work, they've found three times as many male Costa Rican crocs as female ones. They think the reason is a synthetic chemical that got into the crocs' tissues and messed with their

Pesticide mist flies up around a woman spraying a field of lentils. Although she's wearing mouth protection, her eyes and skin are exposed. D SENEESRIYOTA/ DREAMSTIME.COM

Mahmood Sasa and Chris Murray with a male Costa Rican crocodile. The croc has just had blood drawn for testing, and the scientists are taking him back to the lagoon. They work at night because crocs' eyes shine in the dark, making it easier to catch the animals. DAVINIA BENEYTO GARRIGÓS

Many animal babies rely on a parent for their survival. What would happen if endocrine disruptors changed the way this elephant raises its calf. PAULUSSEN/SHUTTERSTOCK.COM

endocrine system—the system that produces and controls an animal's **hormones**.

Hormones are chemicals made in the body and sent in the blood to give a message to another part of the body. When other chemicals enter the blood and start giving messages, the body gets confused. These trickster chemicals are called **endocrine disruptors** because they mimic natural hormones and fool the body.

Endocrine disruptors can cause changes in reproduction, as they did with the crocs, or in behaviors, such as how animals build nests, parent their young, avoid (or not) predators and hunt for food. Sometimes the behaviors sound amusing—seagulls losing their balance, goldfish being hyperactive, macaques (a type of monkey) playing more rough-and-tumble. In reality, though, these behaviors can mean the difference between life and death, and the effects can ripple through whole ecosystems.

My Chemical World

In the 1990s I traveled to New Zealand. After landing, the plane just sat on the runway. Suddenly a fine, whitish mist filled the cabin. It felt cool and moist, as if we were in a cloud. Most people seemed not to notice. Was this normal? The spraying lasted for about 30 seconds. Then nothing happened for several minutes more. Finally the engines restarted, and we headed to the terminal. That was my first (and only) experience with "aircraft disinsection." I learned later that some countries allow aircraft interiors to be sprayed with pesticide to help keep insects and insect-borne diseases from traveling along with human passengers. (New Zealand no longer sprays while passengers are onboard, but some countries still do.)

Along with people, airplanes can transport insects, bacteria, viruses and other unwanted passengers to new places.
CONCEPT PHOTO/SHUTTERSTOCK.COM

WHALES ON DRUGS

All water flows downhill. Okay, fine—that's not much of a news flash. My point is that regardless of whether water is crystal clear or a soupy mix of **pollutants**, it eventually flows into the ocean. Every time it rains in a big seaside city, all sorts of oils, pesticides, industrial chemicals and other pollutants wash over the streets, into storm drains and out to sea, where marine creatures live. Animals can absorb chemicals through their skin and ingest them by drinking polluted water and eating contaminated food.

Remember that group of chemicals I mentioned—industrial chemicals in the PCB group? Well, these chemicals nestle into the fatty tissues that insulate animals from heat and cold. In the ocean, marine mammals such as whales and dolphins have thick layers of fatty tissues called blubber. Some, such as orcas, are also apex predators, so they tend to accumulate high loads of chemicals.

For example, in 2016 a female orca named Lulu died off the coast of Scotland. Scientists tested her blubber and found it had extreme amounts of PCBs. By examining her body, they could also tell that she had never given birth to a calf, even though she was at least 20 years old. Female orcas mature between ages 6 and 10, so why hadn't Lulu had a baby? The high load of contaminants in her body might have made her unable to get pregnant.

POLLUTANTS WITHOUT BORDERS

Europe banned the use of DDT and PCBs in the 1980s. How, then, could an orca in the waters off Scotland become so contaminated?

It turns out these chemicals stay in the environment for a long time. For this reason, they're called **persistent organic pollutants** (POPs). Once they get into the environment,

When water runs over city streets, it picks up pollutants and carries them into streams, lakes or the sea.
ASHADHODHOMEI/SHUTTERSTOCK.COM

Orcas that live in the Salish Sea near my home are under threat. One reason is all the pollution from people living in the region.
MONIKA WIELAND SHIELDS/SHUTTERSTOCK.COM

A submersible named Alvin *has completed another mission to collect samples from the deep sea. The person standing on* Alvin *is helping the pilot, who is sealed inside, steer the submersible back to its ship.* Alvin *hasn't descended into the Mariana Trench, but a few other submersibles have.*
WOODS HOLE OCEANOGRAPHIC INSTITUTE

POPs not only stick around but also move around. Both water and air carry POPs for long distances.

Picture the Mariana Trench, a canyon on the floor of the North Pacific Ocean. Its deepest part is nearly 7 miles (about 11 kilometers) beneath the ocean's surface. Down there, sunlight never filters in, and the temperature hovers just above freezing. Yet even in that remote place, tiny shrimplike animals called amphipods are contaminated. And not just a little bit. Their bodies contain whopping loads of PCB chemicals.

Air currents spread POPs all over the world, taking them from their sources—usually in lower latitudes—to the planet's poles. There the POPs get deposited in the water and on the snow, and they enter the food chain. What happens next? You guessed it. They accumulate in animals and are biomagnified up the food chain to the apex predator, people.

An Inuit family eating traditional foods at their home in Greenland. ARCTICPHOTO.CO.UK

In the high Arctic, many Inuit eat a traditional diet of meat and fatty tissues from seals, belugas, walruses and other animals. Not surprisingly, Inuit mothers' breast milk often contains very high levels of POPs and other contaminants. The chemicals get passed to their babies, whose only food for the first months of life is that milk.

DETERMINED DETECTIVES

If you had been wondering whether POPs and other chemicals can get into humans, you now have the answer. After all, humans are animals too, and the basic way animals' bodies work applies to us as much as to orcas and eagles.

Tracking the effects of chemicals can be tough, though, because they are often delayed and don't become noticeable until years later. Cancer, which can result from exposure to certain chemicals, is an example of an illness that might not show symptoms for many years. Another problem is exposure to many different chemicals. Chemical A and chemical B might have little or no effect on their own, but *together* they might cause a large effect.

The scientists who study the impact of toxic chemicals and pollutants on human health are called *epidemiologists* (epa-DEE-MEE-ol-a-jists). They often look at clusters of people with similar illnesses to trace a common cause. When an outbreak of food poisoning happens and officials warn the public not to eat a certain food, the epidemiologists are hard at their detective work, trying to figure out the cause.

NO LOVE HERE

Midway between Lake Ontario and Lake Erie, in upstate New York, lies a long strip of grass. On satellite maps it looks like a huge playing field with a few paths through it. Zoom in

Even in Antarctica, far from human settlements, persistent organic pollutants (POPs) have been measured in the snow.
WIM HOEK/SHUTTERSTOCK.COM

The children shown in this historical photo are asking to be evacuated from their toxic neighborhood, Love Canal.
BUFFALO COURIER EXPRESS/COURTESY OF THE CENTER FOR HEALTH, ENVIRONMENT AND JUSTICE

and you see gray rectangles adjacent to the strip. The rectangles are the leftover footprints of a demolished school and houses.

In the 1890s a land developer had a canal dug. It was roughly half a mile (one kilometer) long and 20 yards (18 meters) wide. He later abandoned his project, and the Love Canal (named for the developer) sat empty for a few decades. In the 1920s it was put to use as a landfill, receiving 20,000 tons (just over 18,000 tonnes) of city, army and industrial waste. Three decades later the canal-turned-landfill got a top layer of dirt and new life as a green space.

The land next to Love Canal grew into a neighborhood with an elementary school and hundreds of homes. It seemed like any other neighborhood, except for the strange smells in basements and the odd substances that occasionally bubbled up from the ground. Residents complained, but it wasn't until the mid-1970s that air and soil testing and human-health studies began.

My Chemical World

Getting some mountain air after the day spent breathing in San Francisco's car exhaust.
ANGUS RAE

When I was a baby, my parents took me to San Francisco. They spent a whole day pushing me around downtown streets in a low-to-the-ground stroller. By evening I was coughing and wheezing. Was I allergic to something? My parents weren't sure, but it occurred to them that I had spent the entire day at the level of car exhaust pipes, breathing in whatever spewed out. Perhaps my sensitive airways were protesting from the air pollutants they had taken in.

Within a few more years, it became clear that PCBs and other toxic chemicals had leached (leaked and spread) throughout the area's land and water. Officials eventually evacuated the entire neighborhood.

A HEAVY BURDEN

Neighborhood disasters sometimes take years to be recognized, and other times they happen in the blink of an eye.

One of the worst-ever chemical disasters—some say *the* worst ever—happened in 1984 in Bhopal, India. On a December night while people slept, some 44 tons (40 tonnes) of toxic gases leaked out of a pesticide factory and spread through the surrounding communities. The gases—mainly methyl isocyanate, or MIC—burned people's eyes and choked their lungs. Many people died in their beds. Others managed to escape on foot or in cars, but not without breathing in the toxic fumes.

Nobody knows exactly how many thousands of people suffered in this disaster. Even today—three and a half decades later—survivors of that tragic night have ongoing problems with their lungs, eyes, skin, mobility and mental health. Many of the gas survivors have since had children, and they too have physical and mental illnesses.

OUR DAILY DOSE OF CHEMICALS

I know these stories are scary. Could something similar happen where you live? I hope not. But I know something that does happen every day. You eat food, drink water and breathe air. Let's take a closer look at some of the chemicals involved in these universal activities.

A Home-Cooked Meal

You've probably heard the expression "You are what you eat." What *do* we eat?

Activists hold a rally in India on December 3, 2010, the 26th anniversary of the Bhopal disaster.
ARINDAM BANERJEE/DREAMSTIME.COM

A girl smells the soup she and her friends made on their camping trip.
SERGEY NOVIKOV/SHUTTERSTOCK.COM

Bees and other insects do us a huge service by pollinating our food crops. Yet in many parts of the world, pesticides that harm pollinators are still in use.

VLAD SIABER/SHUTTERSTOCK.COM

IT'S ELEMENTAL:
Neonicotinoids, or neonics, are the world's most widely used pesticides. They effectively kill pest insects like aphids. Unfortunately, they also harm bees and other pollinator insects. In 2018 Canada and the European Union announced that they will phase out the outdoor use of neonics and eventually ban them.

In **developed countries**—ones with established industries, a stable government and generally good living standards—people have a huge range of foods available, thanks to large-scale farming. Farmers can grow lots of crops and raise lots of animals quickly and in small spaces. How? By adopting new technologies, using fertilizers and growth hormones, giving animals medicines like antibiotics and—can you guess?—applying pesticides.

When crops are sprayed, some of the chemicals stay on or in the food as **residues** (something that is left behind after a process is complete). People who eat the food ingest those residues. People who live or work in agricultural areas can be exposed twice, first when breathing in chemicals during spraying and again when eating the sprayed food.

It's difficult to figure out the long-term effects of pesticides. Over many years of studies, scientists have found links between pesticide exposure and illnesses like cancer, asthma and diabetes in people around the world.

Plumbing Problems

Here's another contaminant that's harmed people around the world and remains a serious problem today—lead.

Lead is a naturally occurring metal. Its symbol on the periodic table is Pb, from the Latin word for lead, *plumbum*. From this we also get the word *plumbing*. Can you guess one of lead's early uses? Water pipes. Ancient Romans were famous for the aqueducts and channels that brought water to their cities. They funneled water to bathhouses, fountains and homes through pipes, many of them made of lead.

Lead pipes gradually corrode (get weakened and damaged) and leach lead into the water. Over time people drinking that water can get lead poisoning, which damages the brain, heart and kidneys. Lead is especially dangerous for babies and children because it affects brain development, causing behavioral issues and learning difficulties.

None of us live in Ancient Rome, so why worry about lead water pipes? Sadly, cities and builders installed lead pipes all over the world well into the 1900s, and lead solder—an alloy used to join pieces of metal together—was used in plumbing even longer. In many places lead pipes and solder have now been replaced. But lead-contaminated drinking water continues to be a problem for some communities even today. If you want to learn more about the water pipes where you live, contact the water department in your community.

Let's Air It

The Romans kept using lead, despite knowing it caused illness and even death. Ignoring knowledge seems to be a recurring theme in human civilization. In the 1920s American inventor Thomas Midgley Jr. solved the problem of noisy car engines by adding lead to gasoline. Industry-funded scientists declared that leaded gas wouldn't harm the public. But by the 1970s people understood that the lead was causing air pollution. Most countries have since banned leaded gas.

Even so, many air pollutants remain. *Smog* (a word made from "smoke" and "fog") is a serious problem—in 2016, most people (92 percent) lived in places with unacceptable air quality. Air pollution increases cases of asthma—a disease that makes breathing difficult. Asthma is on the rise in cities everywhere. In China the situation is particularly bad, and there's another side effect of the air pollution—fewer people are physically active, probably in part to avoid heavy breathing outdoors, so obesity rates are going up.

Is air quality any better inside? Not always, unfortunately. Cleaning products, art supplies such as markers and glues, and building materials such as plywood can all contain harmful

A child washes her hands under a running tap. Some pipes still leach lead into the water running through them.
GREENAPERTURE/SHUTTERSTOCK.COM

IT'S ELEMENTAL: There's nothing cute about dust bunnies, those loose clumps of dust hiding under the bed. They contain hair, clothing fibers, skin cells, dust mites, pollen, specks of plastic and chemicals like flame retardants, pesticides, plasticizers, metals and more. Time to vacuum!

Playing outside isn't an option for this boy. He wears a mask, even inside his home, to avoid breathing the polluted air.
HUNG CHUNG CHIH/SHUTTERSTOCK.COM

Pesticides keep golf courses free of weeds, but they can also harm wildlife and golfers. A few golf courses are changing their practices by using white vinegar to kill weeds and allowing the odd dandelion to bloom.
DOUBLETREE STUDIO/SHUTTERSTOCK.COM

chemicals that leak into the air. Ever smelled a brand-new plastic shower curtain or a squeezy toy from a dollar store? The strong odor comes from phthalates—chemicals used to soften plastics. They're suspected endocrine disruptors and may also harm the developing brain.

CLEARING THE CLOUDS

I hope you're okay after reading this chapter. You've read stories about terrible things happening to people and the environment. It often helps to talk out loud about scary and upsetting things, so be sure to speak with a teacher, friend or family member if you need to.

I hope that knowing about these things will help you realize that *nobody* is immune to environmental contaminants. Air and water pollution, food contamination and poisonous chemical leaks happen on all seven continents, Antarctica included. And thanks to our connected globe, what happens in one place can affect people and wildlife in other places.

I also hope that these stories will help you consider how we can all make a difference for ourselves, our families and friends, our communities and ultimately our planet. On that note, let me try to clear the clouds with some inspiring stories of success and hope.

IT'S ELEMENTAL: About 17 million babies breathe highly polluted air in their first year of life. Three-quarters of them live in South Asia. Air pollutants affect not just the lungs but also the developing brain.

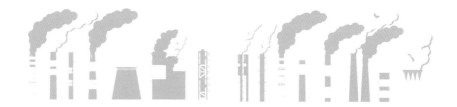

By wearing masks, this family breathes in less of the polluted air on their trip through Ho Chi Minh City in Vietnam.
D BISERKO/DREAMSTIME.COM

CHAPTER FOUR

A Silver Lining

THE HOLE AT THE POLE

Ready for some good news? First up, a global success story. It begins with Thomas Midgley Jr., the inventor who added lead to gasoline. Remember him? Well, his legacy includes unintentionally creating another environmental disaster. He tackled the serious problem of leaky refrigerators. The gases used to cool the inside of fridges in the 1920s often leaked out, with deadly results. Midgley found a solution in a gas he called Freon, which is in the chlorofluorocarbon (CFC) group of chemicals. Freon and other CFCs were stable, didn't cause fires and didn't seem to harm people. CFCs became the go-to gas for refrigerators and air conditioners and also for aerosol spray cans.

CFCs seemed to be nontoxic, at least at ground level. But when they got into the stratosphere—the layer of air that starts about 9 miles (15 kilometers) above the ground and extends to 31 miles (50 kilometers) up—they caused big problems.

Aerosol spray cans used to contain chlorofluorocarbons (CFCs) until people realized that these chemicals destroy ozone in Earth's stratosphere. Many countries have banned CFCs.
JOSEPH SOHM/SHUTTERSTOCK.COM

CFCs destroy ozone, a chemical with three oxygens. Ozone in the stratosphere shields plants and animals on Earth from harmful ultraviolet sunlight. The ozone-damaging effect of CFCs became known in the mid-1970s. In 1985 scientists first detected thinned ozone (dubbed an ozone hole) over Antarctica. Since then ozone holes have been measured elsewhere too.

The world took swift action. Fifty-six countries agreed in 1987 to cut back on CFCs and later banned them. Today the ozone holes are healing.

CHEMISTRY GOES GREEN

Do you hear about "green" this and "green" that all the time these days? The word *green* has come to mean "being sensitive to our planet's health," which, of course, includes human health. Other terms you might see are *earth-friendly, eco-friendly, environmentally friendly, sustainable* and *renewable*. (Unfortunately, some companies claim to be environmentally friendly yet have dubious track records or use harmful practices. Making misleading claims is called *greenwashing*.)

Wind turbines are being installed all over the world. Wind is a renewable energy source.
GISPATE/SHUTTERSTOCK.COM

IT'S ELEMENTAL: Ozone has a double identity. It's helpful in the stratosphere, where it absorbs ultraviolet light. It's harmful in the troposphere—the lowest layer of air, where we are. Here it acts as an air pollutant.

My Chemical World

When I was about nine, my mom gave me my first reusable shopping bag. It was made of strings and could be scrunched up and stuffed in a pocket. My mom explained that when she was a kid, her family never went shopping without their string bags. I used mine to carry all sorts of things, and I still have it! It's one of the many reusable bags my own kids and I use every week when we shop for groceries.

Genevieve carries groceries inside with an assortment of reusable bags, including my decades-old string bag.
ROWENA RAE

37

Observing nature up close helps people understand it and gain inspiration for new inventions.
CGLADE/ISTOCK.COM

If green means being good to the planet, what do you think green chemistry is all about? Yup, it's designing earth-friendly products—ones that aren't poisonous and don't cause pollution. In fact, it's even broader. Green chemistry includes conserving energy, reducing waste and designing products with both their use *and* the end of their useful life in mind. Green chemistry and its cousin green engineering are exciting fields.

Nature often inspires green chemists. Take mussels—these shellfish attach to rocks using a super-strong protein "glue." A green chemist studied this protein and made a similar glue using soy protein. The new glue can replace formaldehyde glues in plywood. Formaldehyde is considered a "probable human ***carcinogen***," meaning it may cause cancer, so replacing it is a good idea.

Looking to nature for ideas is called ***biomimicry***. Nature has been creating and testing things for millennia longer than people have. It makes sense to check out nature's solutions and mimic them or apply them to our many problems.

PICKING PRODUCE PRUDENTLY

I used to hover in my grocery store's produce section, not sure what to choose. Did some fruits and veggies have more pesticide residues than others? Should I buy organic produce? Then I learned about two handy lists published by the Environmental Working Group (EWG). One list ranks fruits and veggies with the most pesticide residues (after being washed and prepared for eating), and the other ranks the cleanest ones.

The top offenders on the Dirty Dozen list for 2019 are strawberries, spinach, kale and nectarines. EWG suggests that growing these foods yourself or buying organically grown ones can reduce the load of pesticides you consume. The stars of the Clean Fifteen list for 2019 are avocados, sweet corn, pineapples and frozen sweet peas. They tend to have few pesticide residues.

Buying fresh fruits and veggies has now become as easy for me as eating them—something we all should do in abundance.

Picking organic strawberries. Yum! SEWCREAM/SHUTTERSTOCK.COM

My Chemical World

I feel fortunate to live where my daughters and I can grow some of our own food. In summer we grow beans, peas, carrots, lettuce, zucchinis, tomatoes and many different herbs. We've also planted blueberry bushes, strawberry vines and four varieties of fruit trees. It's fun to watch things grow and then get the immense pleasure of harvesting and eating the results of our efforts. Best of all, we know our homegrown food is free of chemical pesticides.

My daughters checking out the veggies they helped me plant. ROWENA RAE

LOOKING GOOD

Just like these teens, many people apply five, ten, sometimes more personal-care products to themselves every day. Each product contains numerous ingredients, so the total number of chemicals applied can quickly add up.
ANTONIODIAZ/DREAMSTIME.COM

IT'S ELEMENTAL: Cooking over open fires with fuels like charcoal, wood and dried animal dung (yes, poop!) is a major source of air pollution in some parts of the world. As a result, millions of people get lung disease and other illnesses every year. Since 2010 the Clean Cooking Alliance has been working toward its goal of getting efficient cooking stoves into 100 million homes by 2020.

Did you think I'd forgotten about the question that spurred me to research and write this book—the one about chemicals in my shampoo? Nope, haven't forgotten.

Many shampoos, lotions, nail polishes and other personal-care products—things we put on our skin, hair and nails, and even near or in our mouths (think lip balm and toothpaste)—contain lots of chemicals. Their names are tongue twisters—triclosan, oxybenzone, panthanol, octenylsuccinate…okay, I'll stop!

Several of these ingredients can harm human health. Some are endocrine disruptors. Others cause allergic skin reactions. Some also contaminate the environment.

A few product ingredients are easier to pronounce. Take *fragrance* and *parfum*—they sound good. But are they? It turns out these are catch-all terms for a bunch of chemicals, some known to be endocrine disruptors and some that haven't been tested.

What to do? I found inspiration in a study that teens in Salinas, California, helped design and carry out. One hundred girls ages 14 to 18 stopped using their usual cosmetics, creams and soaps for three days. Instead they used low-chemical products. At the start and end of the three days, they each gave a urine sample, which was tested for several endocrine-disrupting chemicals.

The results showed that in just three days the girls' urine had lower amounts of several chemicals. Some had dropped by a quarter to a third, and one by nearly a half.

That's pretty impressive. We each have the power to reduce the chemicals in our body by choosing which products we use. I've decided to use fewer products, research the ones I do buy and even make a few myself.

Oh, the name of the teens' study? HERMOSA, for Health and Environmental Research in Makeup of Salinas Adolescents. In Spanish, hermosa means *beautiful*.

WHAT CAN ONE PERSON DO?

A lot! And it doesn't matter how old (or young) you are.

Francia Márquez first spoke out for the environment at age 13. Now a mother, she has helped stop illegal gold mining in Colombia. Mining companies were using mercury and cyanide, both highly poisonous, to extract gold. The mining waste flowed straight into the Ovejas River, a drinking-water source for Francia's community. She organized a group of 80 women, who marched 350 miles in 10 days to Bogotá, the capital city, and demanded that the illegal mining be stopped. It took time, but their protest worked, and the mining companies and their machinery left.

At age 11 Stella found out that homes along the LaHave River in Bridgewater, Nova Scotia, where she lives, had pipes going straight from their toilets to the river. Disgusted by this pollution, she tested the river water for a science-fair project and then started campaigning. She got the attention of three levels of government. Local, provincial and federal governments agreed to help 600 homes switch to septic systems. By 2023 the LaHave River will be free of straight-pipe discharge.

Along with some classmates, Nikita, a 12-year-old boy in Kyiv, Ukraine, started a composting project at school. Food waste from their school cafeteria was turned into compost to fertilize trees in their neighborhood. This kept the food waste out of landfills. Named Compola, the project received money to expand into 1,000 other Ukrainian schools.

That's a lot of work for young people who also go to school and have other activities. Even if you can't take on such big projects, you can still do a lot for both your health and the environment's.

Practice Being Skeptical

It's okay not to believe everything you read or hear. Instead ask questions. Get information from different sources—your family,

LeeAnne Walters (left) speaking with people from her hometown of Flint, MI. Walters led a citizens' movement to get Flint's tap water tested for contaminants after the city temporarily switched to a different water source. The testing revealed high amounts of lead. The Flint water crisis started in April 2014.
GOLDMAN ENVIRONMENTAL PRIZE

At age 14, Stella Bowles (blue jacket) visited Sweden to speak about her work. Here she is seen helping other kids learn how to sample water on a river that flows into the Baltic Sea.
ROLAND WIRSTEDT

Lunchtime with reusable containers and wraps. ROWENA RAE

IT'S ELEMENTAL: When plastic food containers get heated, chemicals can leach into the food. Always microwave food in glass or ceramic containers.

Let the dandelions grow too!
PAYA MONA/SHUTTERSTOCK.COM

friends, teachers, books, the internet. Question how trustworthy the sources are. There's a lot of awesome information out there, but there's misleading and inaccurate stuff too.

Read Product Labels

The names on product labels aren't the easiest to pronounce, let alone understand. Even so, you can decide what chemicals you want to avoid and look for products that fit your list. Also explore the online tools and lists that rank different products and foods.

Use Less Plastic Stuff

Plastic pollution has become an enormous global issue, with landfills filling rapidly and garbage patches growing in oceans. Use glass, bamboo or metal products instead of plastic. Beeswax wrapping and cloth bags work great for packed lunches. And you don't really need a plastic straw, do you?

Eat Well

Bring up the idea of buying local and pesticide-free foods with the adults in your life. Plant a garden to grow some of your own food. If you live in an apartment, try container gardening or find out if your neighborhood has a community garden you could join. Grow your plants without using pesticides!

Clean It Up

Research the cleaning products used in your home and talk about replacing them with less toxic ones. For example, a mixture of equal parts water and vinegar makes a great spray cleaner for countertops and windows. Add water to baking soda to make a paste for scrubbing sinks and tubs.

Spread the Word

Talk with family, friends and teachers about chemicals, the environment and health. Challenge them—and yourself—

to switch out some of the products you use or foods you eat for healthier and environmentally safer ones.

Get Active

Join a youth action group, or start your own at school or in your neighborhood. You don't have to tackle a huge part of the chemical contaminants problem. You can focus on one area. For example, you might start a battery recycling program at your school or talk to your neighbors about pesticide-free lawn care.

Think Big, Act Small

Remember, we're all together on this planet—the only one we've got. What we do at home and in our neighborhoods can have an impact far away. Let's treat ourselves, our homes and our communities with the whole world in mind.

When Rupert Yakelashek was 10 and Franny Ladell Yakelashek was 7, they went to city hall in Victoria, BC, to ask for a municipal environmental rights declaration. The city councilors voted in favor of recognizing that all people have the right to live in a healthy environment. Rupert, Franny and others are now working to have more municipalities and even the Government of Canada do the same. SKYE LADELL

Hannah Testa, a teen in Atlanta, GA, is on a mission to raise awareness about plastic pollution and persuade people to use less plastic. Much less. Hannah's organization is Hannah4Change (Hannah4Change.org). FARIDA TESTA

Acknowledgments

My first thanks go to Rachel Carson, an American biologist and author who wrote about science and nature from the 1930s through the early 1960s. When I reread her fourth book, *Silent Spring*, published in 1962, it planted the idea of exploring our current chemical world.

My next thanks go to Merrie-Ellen Wilcox for introducing me to Sarah Harvey, my editor at Orca, who was enthusiastic about my idea from the start and skillfully guided me through writing and revising the manuscript. Thank you, Sarah. Thanks also to Kirstie Hudson and the other fabulous people at Orca who helped bring all the pieces together to form the final book.

I'm very grateful to three reviewers who read the manuscript and pointed out confusing and misleading passages. They are Glenys Webster with Women's, Maternal and Early Childhood Health at the British Columbia Ministry of Health, Victoria, BC; Bruce Lanphear in the Faculty of Health Sciences at Simon Fraser University, Burnaby, BC; and Birgit Claus Henn in the Department of Environmental Health at Boston University School of Public Health, Massachusetts.

Thank you to all the photographers whose photos add so much to the book.

Several friends and colleagues contributed ideas during my research: Carolyn Combs, Winona Met, Michelle Mulder, Lana Okerlund, Frances Peck, Martine Street and Sharilynn Wardrop. Thank you, all.

Special thanks to my daughters, Genevieve and Madeleine, for being willing sounding boards and for living alongside their mother's writing habit.

Resources

Print

Eriksson, Ann. *Dive In!: Exploring Our Connection with the Ocean.* Victoria, BC: Orca Book Publishers, 2018.

Jackson, Tom. *The Elements Book: A Visual Encyclopedia of the Periodic Table.* New York: DK Publishing and Smithsonian Institution, 2017.

Jakubiak, David J. *What Can We Do About Toxins in the Environment?* New York: PowerKids Press, 2011.

Mulder, Michelle. *Every Last Drop: Bringing Clean Water Home.* Victoria, BC: Orca Book Publishers, 2014.

Mulder, Michelle. *Trash Talk: Moving Toward a Zero-Waste World.* Victoria, BC: Orca Book Publishers, 2015.

Wilcox, Merrie-Ellen. *What's the Buzz?: Keeping Bees in Flight.* Victoria, BC: Orca Book Publishers, 2015.

Online

Action for Nature, International Eco-Hero Youth Awards: actionfornature.org

Biomimicry Institute, Youth Design Challenge: youthchallenge.biomimicry.org

Campaign for Safe Cosmetics: safecosmetics.org

Children's Environmental Health Network: cehn.org

Environmental Working Group, Dirty Dozen and Clean Fifteen: ewg.org/foodnews

Environmental Working Group, Skin Deep Cosmetics Database: ewg.org/skindeep

Hannah Testa, environmental activism: hannah4change.org

Little Things Matter: littlethingsmatter.ca

National Institute of Environmental Health Sciences, Kids Environment Kids Health: kids.niehs.nih.gov

Rachel Carson Council: rachelcarsoncouncil.org

Safer Chemicals, Healthy Families: saferchemicals.org

Glossary

alloy—a metal made by combining basic elements in a physical reaction

apex predator—the animal at the top of a food chain

biomagnification—a process by which the concentration of a contaminant increases as the contaminant moves up the food chain

biomimicry—getting ideas from nature for new human technologies

carcinogen—a substance that causes cancer

carnivore—an animal that eats other animals

chemical—a group of basic elements from the periodic table of elements

chemical reaction—a process in which one or more chemicals change into one or more different chemicals

contaminant—a substance that poisons, infects or pollutes something (makes it impure)

developed country—a country with well-established industries and economy, a stable political system and generally good living standards for its people

element—a material that cannot be broken down into anything simpler; there are 118 of these materials, which are grouped on the periodic table of elements

endocrine disruptor—a chemical that interferes with the natural chemicals (hormones) produced by the body

epidemiologist—a scientist who studies patterns of illnesses and diseases in a population of people

food chain—the arrangement of organisms according to feeding relationships, from plants at the base of a chain to herbivores to carnivores

herbivore—an animal that eats plants

hormone—a chemical messenger that travels in the blood to take information to some part of the body

inorganic—anything that is not organic

organic (in chemistry)—something with the elements carbon and hydrogen joined together; includes anything alive or that lived in the past and is now dead

organic (in food production)—food grown and processed without using certain fertilizers, pesticides and hormones

persistent organic pollutant—a harmful chemical that lasts for a long time and travels long distances in the environment

pesticide—a chemical that kills "pests," such as unwanted insects and other animals

petroleum—the liquid "rock oil" or crude oil formed from the remains of millennia-old algae, plants and other organisms; it can be refined into gasoline, plastic and other products

physical reaction—the process of combining two or more chemicals without changing them—you can still get the original chemicals back

poison—any substance that causes illness or death

pollutant—a substance that contaminates the air, water or soil

predator—an animal that catches and eats another animal (the prey animal)

prey—an animal that is food for another animal (the predator animal)

residue—something left behind or remaining after a process is complete

synthetic—something made by humans; artificially made

toxin—a poison that comes from a plant or an animal

toxicant—any poisonous substance, whether natural or synthetic

Index

Index (continued)